IS-250.A: Emergency Support Function 15 (ESF15) External Affairs: A New Approach

By

Fema

5/7/2012

ESF 15: A New Approach to Emergency Communication and Information Distribution

Table of Contents:

Course Overview

The goal of this course is to provide basic training on the concept and practical
application of the ESF 15 Standard Operating Procedures for all FEMA External Affairs
staff (Public Affairs, Office of Legislative Affairs, Community Relations,
Intergovernmental Affairs, International Affairs and Private Sector), regardless of duty
station, as well as to staff in all other agency divisions and federal, tribal, state, local and
Volunteer Organizations Active in Disasters (VOAD) partners.

At the completion of this course, the participant will be able to:

- Explain the purpose of ESF 15 and its relation to External Affairs and the
  National Response Plan (NRP).
- Understand the benefits of integrated and coordinated communications that are at
  the core of ESF 15.
- List the key methods of communication and the key tools used to ensure
  consistency in activation and communications.
- Describe the leadership structure of ESF 15 and the basic responsibilities of the
  seven components that comprise ESF 15.

Lesson 1: Introduction to ESF 15

Lesson Overview

This lesson provides an overview of ESF 15.

Upon completion of this lesson, you will be able to:

- Explain the purpose of ESF 15 and its relation to External Affairs and the National Response Plan (NRP).
- List at least three of the operational elements provided by ESF 15.
- Name the communication protocol used for the transmission of critical and timely incident information among federal, state, local and tribal authorities.
- Explain the phrase and ESF 15 policy: "Talk about what you know and do."

Introduction to ESF 15

Video transcript:

Hello, and welcome to this training of Emergency Support Function (ESF)-15.

Over the course of this presentation, we will take a look at the key components of ESF-15.

We will examine its structure, explore the roles and functions, and discuss the tools that have been created to help Federal, State, and local communicators work more efficiently and effectively together in responding to a crisis. We hope that when we're through, you will have a much better understanding of how ESF-15 functions at both the headquarters and field level.

ESF-15 is the means by which the Federal government will conduct external affairs operations in the event of a crisis. It can also be used as a national model. It will be NIMS Fiscal Year 07 compliant public information. ESF-15 SOPs may also be used as amodel for State external affairs operations.

There will be greater unity among all Federal, State, and local communicators. And there's a national training program underway to educate communicators in the concept. This training will be done for all Federal agencies as well as States and local governments.

It is important to understand that ESF-15 and external affairs operate under the same concept. ESF-15 specifies doctrine and procedures for Federal external affairs activities during a coordinated response.

ESF-15 is a designation or an activation to support a response and recovery effort. The external affairs concept is an operational concept and is the basis on which ESF-15 works. Therefore, ESF-15 and external affairs are guided by the same operating procedures. So exactly what does ESF-15 provide?

Well, first of all, it supports the State, local, and tribal communications effort which is also very important. It creates a unified Federal external affairs team. It also creates a framework from which a coordinated external affairs operation can be successful and, perhaps more importantly, it supports leadership in the field.

ESF-15 has a new approach to the external affairs concept. It is a strategy that is integrated, comprehensive, and empowering. One of the important things about ESF-15 and the new strategy is that it is integrated. It takes all of the external affair components and puts them under one roof working under one single direction.

The ESF-15 External Affairs SOP is in its final review. ESF-15 components are fully incorporated within external processes, and there is improved coordination with all Federal agencies. There is also improved coordination with States, both affected and non-affected.

Primary affected States are incorporated within the national incident communication conference line. There is also coordination through the State incident communications coordination line which helps States talk to States. And there is a training and working partnership that's underway for the external affairs concept.

One other key with the integration is military support coordination and its high priority. There are now strong linkages with Secretary of Defense, Public Affairs, NORTHCOM, Army Corps of Engineers, the National Guard Bureau, and State National Guard staff. ESF-15 is now comprehensive because it brings together all of the external affairs components so they can feed off the strengths of each other.

There is now complete coordination of the Joint Information Center; planning and products; congressional affairs; State, local and tribal affairs, which is also known as intergovernmental; community relations; international affairs; and the private sector.

There is also new visual emphasis throughout all communications opportunities. And, of course, there's a new media access program which provides transparency with stakeholders and all external audiences because we know transparency supports public confidence. It also supports the full Federal-State response effort. Some examples where the new media access program will be most beneficial is when the media is able to follow helicopter rescue crews, urban search and rescue teams, and national Disaster Medical Assistance Teams.

ESF-15 is also comprehensive in some very important ways. Perhaps no way more important than it now provides a detailed concept of operations for both a notice and a no-notice event. It also provides strategic messaging which is designed to identify issues and messages and develop a comprehensive outreach approach. It also has a scaleable organizational chart that can adjust to the size and scope of a response.

There is a Standard Operating Procedure document that now provides a working guide to all Federal, State, and local communicators.

A national training program for Federal agencies is underway and it will also incorporate State communicators and other partners. ESF-15 also ensures that there is timely, accurate, and coordinated communication among all stakeholders. Perhaps one of the most significant items about ESF-15 and the SOP is that it empowers those in the field to make decisions and to conduct the external affairs operation in the field.

ESF-15 field leadership is now authorized to carry out communications to support the Incident Action Plan, the Principal Federal Official, and the Federal Coordinating Officer.

ESF-15 leadership is now empowered. They are authorized and will speak for the PFO and all Joint Field Office functions and Federal Response Actions. Our motto is maximum disclosure with minimum delay.

And there is also a refined media guidance that allows responders to talk to the media. But talk about what you know and what youdo. And we'll explain these concepts a little bit later on.

Lesson Summary

This lesson provides an overview of ESF 15.

You should now be able to:

- Explain the purpose of ESF 15 and its relation to External Affairs and the National Response Plan (NRP).
- List at least three of the operational elements provided by ESF 15.
- Name the communication protocol used for the transmission of critical and timely incident information among federal, state, local and tribal authorities.
- Explain the phrase and ESF 15 policy: "Talk about what you know and do."

In the next lesson, you will learn about ESF 15 activation.

Lesson 2: Collection of Course Features

Lesson Overview

This lesson discusses activation of ESF 15.

Upon completion of this lesson, you will be able to:

- Outline the Operational Authority for overseeing the implementation of ESF 15 in each of the primary ways of activation
- Explain the four primary ways and situations under which ESF 15 can and will be activated
- Define the ESF 15 Concept of Operations and explain who uses it and how it is used
- List the four main ways that ESF 15 daily communications are conducted Rev.

ESF 15 Activation

Video transcript:

When it comes to operational authority, the coordinating agency for any Federal response is the Department of Homeland Security. The primary agency to support that is the Federal Emergency Management Agency. And then you have your support agencies.

Those are all the National Response Plan signatory departments, agencies, and organizations that may be a part of the external affairs operation. But one thing that's important to remember is that when Federal personnel are assigned to the ESF-15 field organization, they will conform to and support the SOP and other policies as directed by the PFO, the FCO, and the JFO SOP.

There are several ways that ESF-15 can and will be activated. There are four primary ways that this can happen. So let me run those down for you.

In an incident of national significance which may include a natural disaster, the DHS Secretary of Public Affairs will direct activation of ESF-15 in coordination with the National Response Coordination Center, the National Operations Center, and FEMA.

There is also a national security special event. When that takes place, the U.S. Secret Service will lead ESF-15 activities for such an event and will designate an External Affairs Officer. In the case that there is terrorism or a law enforcement component to a response, DHS will maintain lead authority over ESF-15. But the FBI and Department of Justice will have lead authority on criminal investigations, and ESF-15 communications activities will be coordinated with those agencies.

The SOP may be modified to reflect the sensitivity of information distribution. And in the event of a radiological incident, once again DHS will maintain overall authority of ESF-15. But the Nuclear Regulatory Commission and the Department of Energy are coordinating agencies that will help with the communication effort.

In order for any ESF-15 activation to be successful, there needs to be consistency in the operation, and that's where the concept of operation comes into play. It's sort of like a playbook on how all of external affairs operations should be conducted.

Here's a brief description of how it's going to work. It is designed to be a daily working external affairs guide for an impending event.

In a notice event, it looks at operations 7 days prior to the event through 5 days following the event. In a no-notice event, it begins at the time the event occurs and goes through 5 days following that event. It is fully scaleable and flexible with respect to the incident situation.

Its main purpose is that it creates a unified planning component that brings unity of effort to all strategic communications planning and product development. The four main components of the concept of operations are the key developments, what has been activated and deployed, the messaging, what are the key messages to convey on that day.

Products. What products need to be created? Press releases, fax sheets to support what that messaging is and actions. What actions should be taken to support the response effort? So you can see that the concept of operations is an important document that's been created to support ESF-15.

One of the key aspects of the ESF-15 SOP and its protocols is how daily communication within external affairs will be conducted on a daily basis and there are four main ways this will be conducted. There is the national incident communications conference line, a State incident communications conference line, a daily event schedule, and a daily communications summary.

Resources

- A sample Activation and Deployment Execution Checklist.
- A sample first page of an actual Concept of Operations for a notice event.
- A Notional Daily Event Schedule.
- A sample Daily Communications Summary.

Lesson Summary

This lesson discusses activation of ESF 15.

You should now be able to:

- Outline the Operational Authority for overseeing the implementation of ESF 15 in each of the primary ways of activation
- Explain the four primary ways and situations under which ESF 15 can and will be activated
- Define the ESF 15 Concept of Operations and explain who uses it and how it is used
- List the four main ways that ESF 15 daily communications are conducted Rev.

In the next lesson, you will learn about ESF 15 management.

Lesson 3: ESF 15 Management

Lesson Overview

This lesson explains ESF 15 Management.

Upon completion of this lesson, you will be able to:

- Explain the primary roles and responsibilities of headquarters leadership within ESF 15.

ESF 15 Management

Video transcript:

So now we've talked a lot about ESF-15 and the SOP and we've discussed things like how is it activated, who's responsible, and what are some of the documents that have been created to help make ESF-15 a successful operation. So I think the best way to start is to take a look at the ESF-15 organizational chart.

And here's what one looks like for a single State event. It's really broken up into two components: a headquarters component and a field-level component. At the headquarters level, of course, the Secretary of the Department of Homeland Security will be the person in charge of catastrophic events. The ESF-15 Director will come out of the DHS Office of Public Affairs, and he/she will assign an ESF-15 Operations Director.

Now, at the field level where most of the action takes place, the Principal Federal Official or the Federal Coordinating Officer will be the person in charge.

Responding to them will be the ESF-15 External Affairs Officer. This is the lead person in the field operation for external affairs. They could have a deputy officer or an executive officer, depending upon the size of the disaster. And there is a resource manager there to help support all of external affairs.

Each component is broken up so that there is a lead person in each one of those components, and they are identified as the Assistant External Affairs Officer for perhaps the Joint Information Center, planning and products, or congressional affairs.

I think it's important that as we move forward, we take a closer look at the ESF-15 headquarters level, who directs that level, what are their responsibilities, and what is the impact on all of the external affairs operations. Of course, the ESF-15 Director is the person that is ultimately in charge of the entire operation.

For all incidents involving ESF-15, the DHS Assistant Secretary for Public Affairs will assume overall leadership of this function.

ESF-15 DHS component directors will coordinate as necessary with the ESF-15 Director. Now, one of the responsibilities of the ESF-15 Director is to assign an Operations Director.

During incidents of national significance, DHS may retain control over this function. In those incidents where FEMA has a lead role, this function will be assigned to FEMA and would typically be assigned to the Director of Public Affairs or the Deputy Director of Public Affairs.

In the event of terrorism or a pandemic, another agency could be assigned this position. This position coordinates with DHS component directors and their staffs and they provide direction, oversight, and coordination to the ESF-15 External Affairs Officer in the field.

The ESF-15 External Affairs Officer is the person that oversees all external affairs operations in the field. They work closely with the Principal Federal Coordinating Officers and they also have a direct reporting structure to the ESF-15 Field Director and the Operations Director. So who appoints them?

They are appointed by the ESF-15 Director who is the DHS Assistant Secretary for Public Affairs. The External Affairs Officer is also known as the ESF-15 Coordinator. He/She manages external affairs resources in accordance with the Incident Action Plan. He/She establishes strategies and tactics to meet objectives with State and local counterparts. He/She oversee the entire external affairs function and establish and communicate basic work procedures.

Resources

- ESF-15 Organizational Chart for a Single State Event.

Lesson Summary

This lesson explains management within ESF 15.

You should now be able to:

- Explain the primary roles and responsibilities of headquarters leadership within ESF 15.

In the next lesson, you will learn about ESF 15 components.

Lesson 4: ESF 15 Management

Lesson Overview

This lesson explains the various components within ESF 15.

Upon completion of this lesson, you will be able to:

- Describe the seven components of ESF 15 in the field and their roles within External Affairs.

ESF 15 Components

Video transcript:

The true key to ESF-15 are the seven components. There's planning and products; the Joint Information Center; Congressional Affairs; Community Relations; State, local, and tribal affairs, also known as intergovernmental; International Affairs; and the private sector.

And we'll start with planning and products, because it is the newest and perhaps the least known of all the functions in the components. Planning and products is the central point for the development of all written external affairs products and internal communications products. In essence, they will support all of the components with their product needs.

Through unity of effort, they centrally direct and develop all strategic planning and messaging from the Joint Field Office. And liaisons provide a coordinated communication link with key program areas and other entities involved in the recovery.

One of the major components of ESF-15 is the Joint Information Center, otherwise known as the JIC. It's established to support and assist in the coordination of Federal, State, local, tribal, and private sector incident communications with the public. It is also the central point for coordination of incident information, public affairs activities, and media access to information regarding the latest developments. It is also the primary location of the media center from which all press briefings will be conducted.

In any joint field office or joint informationcenter, working with the state is critical.

The Federal Coordinating Officer works with the State Coordinating Officer, and in ESF 15 that partnership hooks up with the State Lead Public Affairs Officer and the Assistant External Affairs Officer for the JIC or maybe even Planning and Products.

Together, the staffs from the state and federal agencies will work as a team to convey the most critical information during an incident.

One important function of any type of response is dealing with the media, and not just dealing with the media but who can speak to the media. The ESF-15 Standard Operating Procedures have looked as this issue and come out with new media guidance. Through policy established by the ESF-15 Director, Federal Field Response personnel are authorized to speak to the media within the scope of their assigned duties and knowledge. "Talk about what you know and do". Questions about policy and national decisions are beyond the scope of this and should be referred to an ESF-15 authorized spokesperson. This is not an authorization to solicit interviews or pitch stories, but what we want to do is let the response personnel who are dealing with the issue be able to talk about what they do.

In addition to the media guidance, the ESF-15 Standard Operating Procedure also looks at media access and how that media access can be utilized to best support and capture what responders are doing. The media access program provides transparency for the media by allowing them to review response operations with response teams firsthand. This helps to build public confidence.

Now, there are restrictions that may apply, especially when it comes to national security, law enforcement, privacy, and safety. If any of those are compromised, the media must follow strict guidelines so as not to interfere with the operations.

Now, the media access program is similar to embedding, but typically shorter than the days or weeks associated with media embeds. The media access program is designed for a 1- or 2-day association.

As you can see, visuals are a key element in what ESF-15 Standard Operating Procedures want to accomplish. Some of those key visuals may include such things as satellite imagery, so that we can take a close-hand look at before and after a disaster strikes to see what kind of resources may be needed and the impact on that area. There are GIS products that are produced such as maps and charts that can help convey the severity and the response of any kind of an operation.

And then there is general video that can be used to document the response effort from both the Federal side and the State side.

One thing the ESF-15 SOP emphasizes is visuals over just words. Words only tell so much of the story. But key visuals can provide transparency for what the Federal government and the State government and local government are doing to help citizens in times of need.

Another major component to the ESF-15 structure is congressional affairs. Their primary responsibility is to coordinate the exchange of information between DHS, FEMA, members of Congress, and their staff.

They also respond to congressional inquiries and casework. They arrange for congressional site visits to help members understand the Federal, State, local response, and recovery process. And they develop congressional affairs strategy for outreach and incident-specific objectives.

It would be virtually impossible to carry out an ESF-15 external affairs operation without community relations. They are critical because they provide field outreach to disaster victims and to leaders in their community about Federal and State recovery programs. They have multilingual capabilities that help reach out to communities that may not be in the traditional informational chain.

They implement the speaker's bureau to coordinate public presentations and meetings and they really put a face on Federal and State assistance.

The next component in the ESF-15 external affairs structure is State, local, and tribal affairs, otherwise known as intergovernmental with some agencies.

State, local, and tribal affairs establishes effective working relationships with State, tribal, county, parish, and municipal governments and agencies representing these governments. State, local, and tribal affairs creates and maintains an open two-way line of communication between these groups and FEMA and other Federal agencies.

One of the smaller, but certainly important components to ESF-15, is international affairs, particularly in the event of a catastrophic event where there is a lot of foreign interest. International Affairs coordinates all foreign delegation visits by providing informational briefings and site visits to impacted areas. They liaise with the department of State on all international activities including donations of goods and services, and they assist with the coordination of foreign press, working with the foreign pss center at the Department of State.

The last component in the ESF-15 structure is one of the newest and one of the most unique, and that is the private sector. The >private sector is responsible for coordinating with established business networks and industry-specific-related groups such as the U.S. Chamber of Commerce, other national networks, and State and regional networks.

Their primary responsibility is to identify issues that directly affect the private sector and the business community. They coordinate with businesses to reach out to employees on recovery programs. The private sector component is coordinated by DHS.

Resources

- ESF-15 Planning & Products Organizational Chart.
- ESF-15 Joint Information Center (JIC) Organizational Chart.
- ESF-15 Congressional Affairs (CA) Organizational Chart.
- ESF-15 Community Relations (CR) Organizational Chart.
- ESF-15 Intergovernmental: State, Local & Tribal Affairs (IGA) Organizational Chart.
- ESF-15 International Affairs Organizational Chart.
- ESF-15 Private Sector Organizational Chart.

Lesson Summary

This lesson explains the various components within ESF 15.

You should now be able to:

- Describe the seven components of ESF 15 in the field and their roles within External Affairs.

In the next lesson, you will learn about ESF 15 Execution.

Lesson 5: ESF 15 Execution

Lesson Overview

This lesson explains the four phases of ESF 15 execution.

Upon completion of this lesson, you will be able to:

- List the four phases of ESF 15 execution and explain when each phase begins
- Describe the primary actions that occur in each of the four phases of ESF 15 execution

ESF 15 Execution

Video transcript:

So let me try to wrap all of this up for you by showing you an execution phase and action chart using an advance notice event and a no-notice event, showing how the ESF-15 components and all of the concepts that we've discussed work together.

In the case of an advanced notice event, we start with the awareness phase. This is where ESF-15 is activated. State and local contacts are made and the initial planning is started and the concept of operations is now activated. As we move to the readiness phase, ESF-15 leadership is now deployed and the ESF-15 functions are activated.

There is a proactive State, local, and Federal communications plan that is developed. Some of the primary messages may include final preparedness actions, self-sufficiency for up to 72 hours, supporting State and local instructions pertaining to issues such as evacuation and sheltering, and certainly defining the Federal response.

When the event occurs, we then go into the response phase. This is where a unified State, local, and Federal response picture is defined. The media access with responders is now initiated, providing transparency in the operations, and some of the primary messages are life-saving and life safety information.

Federal support and capabilities that are being provided to State and local officials, and they establish realistic expectations for FEMA and other Federal assistance programs. Once the response phase transitions into the recovery phase, we have a fully-integrated external communications effort through ESF-15, where we amplify and identify the recovery priorities and the primary messages focus on supporting State recovery efforts, demonstrating and showing recovery and support material, and being proactive with consistent information on Federal assistance programs.

We hope by reviewing the four phases of a potential event you can see how all of the components of ESF-15 and the concepts that we've discussed come together to form an effective external affairs campaign. By integrating all the external affairs components into a single Emergency Support Function, ESF-15, we are able to provide a more comprehensive outreach effort.

By empowering ESF-15 staff as well as responders in the field, we can offer a unified message that meets the needs of Federal, State, local, and tribal partners and communicates essential information clearly and concisely to individuals and communities working to recover and rebuild.

We hope this presentation has been informative and has given you a better understanding of how the ESF-15 Standard Operating Procedure should work. We all know the importance of external affairs and we appreciate you taking the time to learn more through this training.

Resources

- List of key actions at each execution phase.

Lesson Summary

This lesson explains the four phases of ESF 15 execution.

You should now be able to:

- List the four phases of ESF 15 execution and explain when each phase begins
- Describe the primary actions that occur in each of the four phases of ESF 15 execution